Kids' Easy Guide to Painting

Learn to Paint **Ladybug**, **Caterpillar**, **Butterfly**, **Turtle**, **Snake**, **Whale**, **Tulip**, **Rose** & So Much More

BY

Hax Shannon

Copyright © 2018 – **Lost River Publishing House**

All Rights Reserved.

No part of this publication may be reproduced, stored in a retrieval system or transmitted in any form or by any means, electronic, mechanical, photocopying, recording or otherwise without the proper written consent of the copyright holder, except as permitted under Sections 107 & 108 of the 1976 United States Copyright Act, without the prior written permission of the publisher.
Lost River Publishing House publishes its books and guides in a variety of electronic and print formats, Some content that appears in print may not be available in electronic format, and vice versa.

Cover design & Layout

Susanne Rothman
First Edition

HERE IS WHAT'S IN THIS BOOK

Here is what's In This Book 3
Introduction to rock painting 4
Supplies You will Need 5
Mixing colors 10
How to paint a ladybug 12
How to paint a caterpillar 19
How to paint a butterfly 25
How to paint a rocket ship 33
How to paint the planet Saturn 38
How to paint stars 41
How to paint a turtle 45
How to paint a lizard 51
How to paint a snake 57
How to paint a starfish 63
How to paint a clownfish 68
How to paint a whale 72
How to paint daisies 77
How to paint a tulip 80
How to paint a rose 83
Painting spots 89
Painting stripes 91
Painting zigzags 93
Conclusion 95

INTRODUCTION TO ROCK PAINTING

When you are out walking in the park or down the street, do you ever look around and wonder "what if there were a bunch of sea creatures who live here? What if I was on the moon? What if there were lots of ladybugs hiding in the bushes?" With the magic of rock painting, you can add all sorts of fun critters and colors to any environment!

In this guide I'll go over some basic supplies and steps to getting started in rock painting. I'll show you how to paint all sorts of designs step-by-step, and end sections with some brainstorm prompts to help you come up with your own ideas!

Painting is a great, creative way to decorate, express yourself, and have fun. Let's get started by looking at some supplies!

SUPPLIES YOU WILL NEED

Here is a list of supplies you will need:

- Rocks
- Acrylic paint (I recommend getting the colors red, yellow, blue, black, white)
- Paint brushes (small, medium, large)
- A rag, cloth, or paper towel that you don't mind getting paint on
- A container for water
- Your imagination!

Now I'll go through each one on the list.

Of course, for rock painting you're going to need rocks.

You can gather rocks a backyard, or the park, or the beach. Are there other places you can think of to gather rocks from?

Important: when you're going out into the world to look for rocks, make sure you check with an adult first. They can probably help you, and let you know which rocks

are okay to take.
You can also find rocks specially made for crafting at craft supplies stores, or online. If you need help, ask an adult!

Next you'll need paint! **Acrylic paint** is a really good choice for rocks. Acrylic paint is plastic-based, and when it's dry, it'll be waterproof and stay on your rock for a long time.

There are lots of options for acrylic paints that come in lots of colors! Here's a picture of the kinds of paints I'm planning to use in this book.

If you need some help getting paint, ask a grown-up for help buying acrylic paint.

You might want to get lots of different colors. But did you know that you can mix most colors using red, yellow, and blue?

I recommend starting with these colors: red, yellow, blue, white, black. In the last section of this part of the guide, I'll explain how to mix colors!
First, let's talk about paint brushes.

You can find paint brushes at almost any art supply store, or online. I recommend getting several different sizes paint brushes. Small paint brushes work well for fine details, like painting eyes and faces. Bigger paint brushes are good for filling in colors, or for painting an entire rock one color. Middle-sized paint brushes are good for things like coloring. Use the brush that you like the best!

Rocks can be a little dirty, and paint can get messy, so it's also good to have a rag or some paper towel with you.

I decided to use a rag. Make sure it's one that you don't care about!

Important: Acrylic paint does **not** come out of fabric. If you aren't sure, ask a grown-up if they have a rag that would be okay to use. Or you can always use paper towel.

Before you start painting your rocks, it's a good idea to quickly wipe them down with your rag to get rid of any dirt or other funky stuff.

You'll also need a container for water! I like to use a small glass jar.
Here's what my full setup looks like.

Alright! Now that you have everything you need, we can get started!

MIXING COLORS

I mentioned earlier that the best colors to have when you're painting are blue, yellow, red, white, and black.

You can take a look at how I mixed some colors together!

Yellow and red make orange.

Yellow and blue make green.

Red and blue make purple. Add a little bit of white to make it a nicer shade of purple.

Adding white to colors make them lighter. For example, on the right I mixed white and red for pink, blue and white for light blue, and yellow and white for light yellow. You can always experiment on paper before you paint your rock. Try mixing green and light blue. What color do you get? What if you mix more yellow into orange? Color is a fun puzzle and there's lots of ways to put things together.

Now that you have some materials, let's get started painting rocks!

HOW TO PAINT A LADYBUG

Ladybugs are very friendly critters. And, it's really easy to paint a rock to look like a ladybug!

First, let's pick out our rock that we'll paint to look just like a cute little ladybug.

Ladybugs are small, round, and slightly oval-shaped. Out of this batch of rocks, the middle one looks like the best choice!

Here's our ladybug rock! Before you get started, it's a good idea to wipe down your rock and make sure it's clean.

I'm using a rag to clean off my rock. You could use a rag, a towel, a paper towel, a sock, whatever you have lying around that you don't mind getting a little dirty!

Alright, now that our rock is clean and ready to be painted, let's start by painting it completely white.

The reason it's good to paint it white to start is so that all your colors show up nice and bright!
You can paint the entire rock, or just the top if you like.

Before you move onto the next step, make sure the white paint has completely dried!

Next we'll paint it red, just like a ladybug!

Next we'll add some details, like a head!

To make the head, paint a little half-circle at the bottom of the rock, where you want the head to be. Use the color black, to match the colors of a ladybug.

Next we'll add a line down the back to show the wings!

Good job! You can see how the ladybug design is coming together, and it fits the rock shape really well. I bet yours looks really good so far!

Next we'll add one of the most important parts of any ladybug, the spots!

To make ladybug spots, paint three black circles on each wing.

You can copy my spots if you like, and maybe on your next ladybug rock, you can add whatever kinds of spots you like!

Now that the black head is nice and dry, we'll go ahead and add some white eyes.

Paint two white circles on the head.

Our ladybug friend is almost complete!

Let the white paint dry. Next we'll add a couple more details, and then our ladybug pal will be complete!

Paint two black dots on the eyes for pupils, and two short black lines coming off the head for its antennas.

Congratulations! You've just make your very first rock painted rock!

This little ladybug would love to keep the flowers in your garden company. Or maybe she wants to hang out in your room on your desk! Where do you plan to let your little ladybug live?

HOW TO PAINT A CATERPILLAR

Caterpillars are amazing animals. They start out as cute little worms and then they grow into beautiful butterflies.

Let's figure out a good shape rock for our caterpillar. Since caterpillars are long and worm-shaped, it'd be good to pick out a long oval rock!

I think the bottom rock gives me the most space to make a cute little caterpillar. Let's paint a white circle for the head:

Let your white circle dry.

Next we'll keep adding white circles until we have a nice long caterpillar:

Two circles!

Three circles!

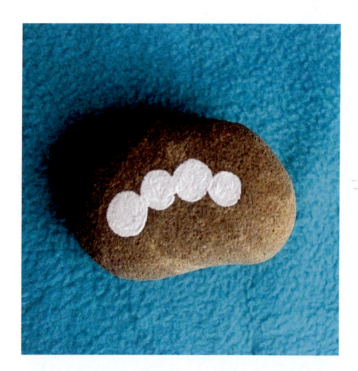

Four circles!

Five circles!

Okay, now we have a nice long caterpillar.

Our caterpillar wouldn't be complete without some antenna, though! Let's add two short lines coming out of the head.

Now we're ready to add color!

Before you add color to your caterpillar, make sure to let all of the paint white completely dry. It should be dry to the touch.

I decided to mix a little bit of white paint with my green paint to make a nice light green for my caterpillar. Let's start by painting all the circles:

Nicely done! Our caterpillar is nearly complete.

Next, let's add some color to the antenna. I'm going to paint them yellow.

Very good!

Now we'll add some details to the face, to give our caterpillar a little personality. Caterpillars each a whole bunch, which can make them pretty sleepy. Don't you get sleepy after a big meal?

To make a sleepy caterpillar, paint two curved lines, and a little smiling mouth:

You did it!! Now you have a sleepy caterpillar friend.

What makes caterpillars so magical is that they turn into butterflies. In the next section I'll show you how to paint your own butterfly, to be friends with this nice caterpillar!

HOW TO PAINT A BUTTERFLY

Butterflies are one of the prettiest insects. Their wings come in all kinds of colors and sizes. In this part of the book, I'll show you how to paint a butterfly!

Let's look at some rock shapes and decide which one would be good for a butterfly.

Unlike the ladybug, for this design we'll just paint onto a rock, instead of painting the whole rock.

Since butterflies have such pretty wings, I want to make sure I pick out a rock that gives me a lot of room to paint some wings. I'll go with the bottom rock out of this group.

First things first: the head! Paint a single white single in the middle of your rock. This will be your butterfly's head!

Next, we'll add some white circles to our circle to make the eyes.

You can also think of the eyes as adding half circles onto each side of the head.

Next, let's paint the body.

Paint a long, skinny oval that comes down from the head.

Now you have the head, eyes and body of your butterfly ready to be colored!

Next, we'll paint on the wings. Every butterfly needs some pretty wings!

A butterfly wing can be broken up into two parts: the top and the bottom. To start, we'll paint the top of each wing.

Starting at the body, you'll paint a rounded triangle shape, just like how I did in the picture.

But our poor butterfly won't be able to fly very far with just the top parts of wings! Next we'll paint on the bottom section of each wing.

You can think of the bottom part of each wing as a half-oval.

We're almost done with our white base! But what butterfly would be complete without some antennas?

To add antenna to your butterfly, paint some lines that come out of the head, just like this:

Alright! You're doing such a good job! Now that our white outline is done, we get to add some fun colors!

To get started, we'll paint the head and body. I decided to use a light purple:

I decided to paint my butterfly's body a nice light purple.

Now we'll add some color to the wings!

I painted the top part of my butterfly's wings a nice yellow. In fact, I thought it was such a nice color I decided to paint the antenna yellow too! Let's go ahead and paint the antenna now.

Butterflies look so much better in color don't they?

We're getting pretty close to finishing out butterfly! Let's color the bottom wings now.

I painted my butterfly's bottom wings a nice orange. Next I'll add some spots to the top wings. To make the design feel nice and balanced, I'm going to use the same color orange in the top wings to add some spots:

What a beautiful butterfly! I bet your butterfly looks really good, too!

We're almost done. Before we finish up, let's add a little bit whiter to the eyes, to make two white ovals on the head.

Make sure you let everything get nice and dry before we move onto the last step.

Now all we have to do is add the pupils to the eyes, and a little mouth.

I'm going to paint them on in the color black, just like this:

Ta-da! Now you have a little butterfly rock. Maybe your butterfly wants to hang out with some flowers, or near your front door, so he can say hello to all your friends!

HOW TO PAINT A ROCKET SHIP

Have you ever wanted to bring a little bit of outer space to Earth? In this section we'll paint some rocks that are out of this world!

In order to blast off into the stars, you'll need a trusty rocket ship of course! That's what we'll paint in this section.

Let's take a look at some rocks and pick out a good shaped-rock for a rocket ship.

Rocket ships shoot upwards towards the sky, so a tall oval-shaped rock will work really well. I'm going to use the top rock.

First, paint the body of the rocket ship in white paint. The body of a rocket ship is kind of triangle-shaped, like this!

Alright! Now we'll need to add some fins so our rocket can steer through space. Paint two triangles at the base of your rocket, just like this:

Next we'll add the motor at the bottom.

And we'll also add some flame to send our rocket ship up into space!

Now that our white outline is done, make sure you let it completely dry before moving on to the next step. Letting paint dry is always important to do!

I decided to color my rocket ship gray.

After letting the body dry off, I'll paint the fins red.

I added an extra fin to the middle of the bottom of my ship, just above the engine.

Now let's add some color to that flame! I painted my flame yellow:

Our rocket ship is nearly ready to blast off!

To finish it up, I'm going to paint the engine black and add a red cone to the top.

Alright! Now we're ready to explore the beauty of space!

HOW TO PAINT THE PLANET SATURN

In this section I'll show you how to paint the planet Saturn! Saturn is a very iconic planet and a very popular space design. I'll be perfect for a rock.

Saturn is round with a ring around it. I think any of these rocks would be a good rock for Saturn. I think I'll go with the top-right rock this time.

First, paint a white circle in the middle of the rock.

Now we'll color the planet.

I painted my Saturn planet orange.

Now make sure you let your color dry before doing the next step.

I'll show you how to paint the ring around Saturn. You'll paint it so that it goes over the planet, to give it the appearance of going all the way around.

First you'll paint the ring in white. Let the white dry, and now let's add the color.

Ta-da! You have your very own Saturn now. This one you can hold in your hand! The real Saturn is way too big for that.

What other planets can you think of to paint?

HOW TO PAINT STARS

What night sky would be complete without some twinkling stars?

You can grab any kind of rock to decorate with stars. Here's some that I was looking at:

I think I'll take the rock in the top left.

I'm going to paint a few stars onto my rock.

I'll start with just one.

When I paint a star, I start with my brush in the middle, and paint outwards. This way I can make the five points, and fill it in to make it thicker if I want to. I'm going to add a couple more.

I like to cover most of the rock with stars so it looks like a full night sky.

Alright! Now it's time to color. You can make your stars any color you like. I'm going to make mine pink, green, and what fun! Stars are fun to decorate and can add a little bit of space magic to any scene.

That's our space rocks!

What other space designs can you think of? Here's some ideas that I'll share with you!: paint a comet, paint the planet Jupiter, paint the sun and the moon… the possibilities are endless!

HOW TO PAINT A TURTLE

Next time you're outside, keep an eye out for some scaly slithering friends. In this section we'll learn how to paint some reptiles!

To get started, I'll show you how to paint a turtle!

I chose to pick out a nice round shape for my turtle.

First, paint an oval in the middle of your rock for the turtle's shell.

Now add a half-circle to the top for the head.

Alright! Now we'll add some legs. This turtle isn't hiding in its shell!

Paint four half-circles on each side of the shell:

Lastly, add a little triangle at the bottom for the tail!

Now it's time to color!

First, color the shell. I decided to color my turtle shell green.

Next, paint color the head, legs, and tail.

Make sure your rock is completely dry before moving on to the next step.

Let's decorate our turtle shell with some spots! Before you pick a color, paint the spots on in white.

Once your white spots are dry, you can add the color! I decided to give this turtle pink spots.

Now you can add two black dots to the head for eyes.

One turtle ready to go!

Let's make some friends for the turtle!

HOW TO PAINT A LIZARD

Let's look at some rocks and figure out which shape would be good for a lizard.

Lizards are long and have legs that can stretch out away from their bodies. I'm going to pick a long rock with a lot of room on it for the lizard's body and legs.

Perfect!

First, paint an oval in the middle of the rock for the body.

Next, paint on its head at the top. The head looks like this:

Now add the tail to the bottom. I gave my lizard a thick tail, so that it looks like a gecko! It looks like this:

Now you'll add the legs. Add two legs on each size of the body. Paint on the legs by painting short white lines:

Now it's time to add the toes! At the tip of each leg, paint three short lines:

Great job! Next we'll add some colors.

I painted my entire lizard purple. Make sure you let it dry before moving on to the next step.

Let's add some patterns and spots to our lizard! Paint them on in white first and let it dry. I gave my lizard stripes and spots.

While we're at it, let's add the eyes two. Add two circles to the head like this:

Now time for more colors!

I painted all my lizard's decorative scales and eyes yellow.

Now just add two dots to the eyes for its pupils:

Awesome! Now your turtle has a scaly-friend.

There are lots of lizards in the world, in all different sizes and colors. What kinds of lizards can you think of to paint next?

HOW TO PAINT A SNAKE

Snakes are really neat animals. Unlike lizards and turtles they don't have any legs!

They get around by using muscles on their tummy to scoot along.

Since snakes are long and windy, keep an eye out for a long rock.

Out of this batch I'm going to use the one on the bottom!

First, paint the head. Paint a small oval near the bottom of the rock:

Next paint the body. Snakes are long and slithery, so I'm going to paint a long bendy body like this:

Great job! You can make your body longer if your rock is really long, and really bendy if you have a lot of room to fill in.

Now paint on that little tongue!

Now it's time to color!

I'm going to give my snake stripes, so I'm going to start with one color but leave some white gaps to fill in with the next color.

That looks just like this:

I chose red.

Next I'm going to add yellow!

Once that dries, color the tongue.

Time to add the eyes!

Paint two narrow ovals on the head. I decided my snake's eyes are green.

Once that dries, add a black line to the middle of each eye to add the pupil.

Now this snake is ready to slither away!

Snakes can have all sorts of patterns. You could paint a snake with spots, or with vertical stripes. You could even paint a snake in all the colors of the rainbow!

HOW TO PAINT A STARFISH

Do you ever wonder what lives at the bottom of the ocean? In this section I'll show you how to paint sea critters on your rocks!

We'll start with a starfish!

I'm going to use the bottom rock here.

A starfish has five arms. Let's start by painting the first arm. Paint a white triangle near the middle of your rock.

Next we'll paint the next arm. Paint another triangle that connects to the first one.

Great job!

Do it once more for the next leg. You can also fill in the middle of the starfish at this step, just like this:

Now add the right arm.

Now paint the bottom right arm!

Let the white completely dry before moving onto the next step.

Time to add color!

I decided to paint my starfish pink.

You can decorate your starfish if you like! I'm going to add some orange spots on mine.

Lastly, use some black paint and a thin paintbrush to paint on a little face.

Great job!

Can you think of some other expressions you'd like to paint onto a starfish?

Maybe you want to paint a yellow happy one, a blue sad one, or a goofy purple on!

HOW TO PAINT A CLOWNFISH

Clownfish are super cute. In this section I'll show you how to paint one!

First let's look at some rocks.

Clownfish are small and oval-shaped, so I picked a nice small oval rock for mine.

Paint a white oval in the middle of your rock for the body.

Next paint on the tail by painting a half-circle at the end of the body.

Now add some more fins!

Paint two more smaller half-circles on the top of the body. Try to make the left one little bigger than the right one.

Great!

Now it's time to color it!

Clownfish are orange. Paint the whole fish orange.

Now let that dry!

Let's paint its white stripes back on.

It's coming together!

Now I'm going to paint on a little smiley face using black paint.

Almost done!

Clownfish have some black on the tips of their fins. That looks like this:

Excellent job!

Can you think of any other kinds of fish you'd like to paint? You could make a whole school of fish for your clownfish!

HOW TO PAINT A WHALE

Whales are the biggest creatures on the planet! So we're going to need a big rock!

Out of this group of rocks I'm going to use the one on the top right.

First paint a circle in the middle of your big rock.

Next you'll paint a small curved triangle at the end for the tail.

At the tip of the tail, paint two skinny ovals for the fins.

Now let it dry!

I'm going to paint the body of my whale blue. To make the whale's color pop I painted the rest of the rock with a light yellow color, but it is optional, you don't have to do it, if you don't want to.

Let's add some details, like water coming out of a blowhole!

Using a darker blue, paint three lines near the top of the head.

Now our whale is taking a breath of fresh air!

I'm going to give my whale a light blue tummy. Add some light blue along the body of your whale's body, just like this:

Now it's time for the finishing touch: adding a face! Using black and a thin paintbrush, add a dot for the eye and a little smiley face.

Awesome!

There's lots of animals that live in the sea. Can you think of some more ideas? Maybe you want to paint an octopus, or seal, or even a giant squid!

The possibilities are as vast as the sea!

HOW TO PAINT DAISIES

Daisies are a cute and fun decorative flower that you could easily add to any rock. If fact, if you wanted to, you could go back and add daisies to all sorts of designs we've done in this book. Maybe the butterfly you made would like some daisies!

I'm going to use the top rock out of this group to decorate with daisies.

First, paint three paint spots. You want to space them out because you will add the petals next.

Alright! Now we'll add the petals. From each dot, you can paint out the petals using your paintbrush.

You're almost done! Daisies are a pretty easy design. That's one thing that makes them so fun!

I added yellow spots to the middle of each of my daisies.

And there you have it!

Can you think of other colors you would like to paint your daisy? Next time feel free to experiment! Maybe you want to paint a rock covered in daisies of every color of the rainbow!

HOW TO PAINT A TULIP

Next we'll paint a tulip!

Tulips stand nice and tall, so I'm going to pick a tall rock for my tulip.

First, paint a white line in the middle of your rock. Then, paint two leaves at the bottom of the stem.

Very good! It's coming together!

Next paint the top of the flower. That should look like this:

Great!

Now let all the white paint dry.

I'm going to paint my stem and leaves green. Color the stem and leaves like this:

Time to paint the flower now! I'm going to paint mine a nice bright red.

Congratulations! You did it!

In no time you'll have your very own flower garden!

HOW TO PAINT A ROSE

Roses are red... and pink, and purple, and green, and rainbow-- roses are any color you want to make them when you're painting them!

Let's look at some rocks.

Roses stand long and tall, just like a tulip. I'll use the rock in the bottom right corner for a rose.

First, paint a white line down the middle of your rock.

Next, add the leaves. I decided to add one leave to each side of the stem. That looks like this:

There you go!

Now let's paint the flower. Paint a shape at the top of the stem that looks like this:

Now make sure you let all your white paint dry!

Next we'll paint the stem and leaves. I decided to make my rose have a light green stem and leaves.

Now paint the flower. I'm going to use pink.

Now, roses have a center to them, where all the petals come out from. To paint the middle, mix some white into whatever color you chose to make your rose. Because I used pink, I'm going to add some white to make a very light pink. Then, you'll paint a shape in the middle. It looks just like this:

Next, I'm going to add some highlights with the same color. Follow the picture below as a guide:

Last but not least, I'm going to add some white details to the middle of the rose. Use the picture below as a guide:

You did it!

Can you think of any other flowers to paint? Maybe a daffodil, or a violet, or some snapdragons!

You could even paint more daisies, tulips, and roses in sorts of colors. Whatever you dream up, you can make!

PAINTING SPOTS

Sometimes it's just fun to play with colors and shapes. In this section, we'll experiment painting our rocks solid colors and decorating them!

First let's start with polka dots!

I decided to paint my rock completely purple.

Let it dry!

Now, you can decorate it with spots however you like. Make sure to paint the spots in white, so the next color shows up much brighter!

Great! I think yellow spots would be really fun to have on this rock, so I'm going to paint them yellow!

Nicely done! This spotted rock kind of looks like a dragon egg! Can you think of other magical things you could decorate a rock to look like?

PAINTING STRIPES

Stripes are another fun way to decorate a rock.

To start, I painted my rock completely white. Then, I added some horizontal stripes in green. You can choose any color you like!

Great! Now you can fill in the other stripes with another color if you want! I'm going to do pink!

This rock looks like a piece of watermelon!

What else could you do with stripes on a rock? What other colors could you use? You could paint each stripe a different color if you like!

PAINTING ZIGZAGS

Zigzags are another fun pattern to paint. To start, pick any rock you like, and paint it all white. I'm using a really big rock!

Next, add the zigzag stripes. You can use this picture as a guide. I decided to make my zigzags red.

To finish it up, I'm going to paint the rest of the zigzags black!

You did it!

Did you know you could combine spots, zigzags, and stripes? Try it out! Feel free to experiment with all kinds of colors. If you feel like it, paint a rock a solid color and leave it at that. Add spots if you want!

Can you think of other shapes to paint onto a rock? You could add spirals, triangles, squares… The possibilities are limitless! Experiment and have fun!

CONCLUSION

I hope you enjoyed following along with the designs in this book! But don't feel limited to what you learned here. You can use your imagination to come up with all sorts of ideas.

There are lots of ways to decorate, and now that you have a hang of the basics, you can experiment and explore. Try mixing new colors! If you have glue and googly eyes or glitter, try adding some final touches to your rocks. See what works!

Thanks for painting!

Made in the USA
Middletown, DE
24 June 2019